Angelina Ballerina

My First Cookbook

This book belongs to:

LONDON, NEW YORK, MUNICH,
MELBOURNE, AND DELHI

Project Editor Lindsay Fernandes
Designer Lynne Moulding
Recipe Consultant Fiona Munro
Photographer Dave King
Home Economist Sarah Tildesley
Publishing Manager Simon Beecroft
Brand Manager Lisa Lanzarini
Art Director Mark Richards
Category Publisher Alex Allan
Production Rochelle Talary
DTP Lauren Egan

First published in Great Britain in 2005 by Dorling Kindersley Limited,
80 Strand, London WC2R 0RL
A Penguin Company

05 06 07 08 09 10 9 8 7 6 5 4 3 2 1

A CIP catalogue record for this book is available from the British Library.

ISBN 1-4053-1143-6

Reproduced by Media, Development and Printing, Ltd., UK
Printed and bound in China by Hung Hing

Discover more at
www.dk.com

Contents

Before you begin

I love cooking, and the recipes in this book are for my favourite tea-time treats that are perfect for parties! All good cooks follow a few simple rules to make sure that cooking is safe and lots of fun, so make sure you read them before you start cooking!

Read the rules carefully!

Ask for help

You should always have an adult with you when you are cooking. It is especially important for an adult to help you with the steps marked with a hand symbol.

I always ask my Dad for help with the oven.

Be prepared
Take time to read the recipe from the start to the end carefully so that you are ready for each of the steps.

Tie your hair back
Remember to tie your hair back when you are cooking, so you can see what you are doing – and so your hair doesn't fall into the food!

Keep clean

Cooking can be messy so remember to wear an apron and roll up your sleeves to keep your clothes nice and clean.

Wash your hands

You must have clean hands when you are cooking so you don't spread any germs. Always wash your hands carefully before and after cooking.

Oops – don't dance in the kitchen!

Take care

Pay attention to what you are doing in the kitchen – you don't want to spill things or hurt yourself!

Have fun!

Remember to have fun when you are cooking. Don't worry if your food doesn't look perfect. It will still taste nice and you will enjoy sharing yummy treats with your friends!

I'm good at
helping Mum.

Jewel biscuits

It's fun baking in the kitchen with my
Mum. My cousin Henry loves to bake too,
but he can be a bit messy! I help Henry to
make biscuits in lots of different shapes.
We can't wait to taste them!

To make 15 biscuits you will need:

★ 60g (2oz) plain flour
★ 30g (1oz) butter
★ 30g (1oz) caster sugar
★ 1tbsp beaten egg

1. Ask an adult to turn on the
oven to 180°C (350°F/Gas 4).

2. Sieve the flour into a bowl and,
using your fingers, rub in the butter
until there are no lumps.

3. Stir in the sugar
and the beaten egg.
Now use your hands
to form the mixture
into a firm dough. Add a
little more egg if you need to.

4. Sprinkle some flour onto a clean worktop and use your hands to knead the dough until smooth.

Dancers need food for energy.

5. Roll out the dough until it is around 3mm thick. Now cut out pretty shapes using biscuit cutters.

6. Put your shapes on a non-stick baking sheet and ask an adult to place them in the oven for 12 minutes, or until golden.

When they are ready, ask an adult to take them out of the oven and leave them to cool.

Now turn the page!

To decorate your biscuits you will need:

★ 60g (2oz) icing sugar
★ 1tbsp water
★ Food colourings

Your biscuits are ready to decorate when they are completely cold.

1. Sieve the icing sugar into a bowl. Gradually add the water until you have a smooth icing that coats the back of a spoon thickly.

2. Put a small amount of the icing into several different bowls. Add a drop of a different colouring to each bowl and stir until the colours are even.

3. Now decorate your biscuits using a teaspoon or palette knife. Covered in pretty pastel icing, they will look like fabulous precious jewels!

Make your icing the same colours as our tutus.

I can't wait for a nibble!

For a really personal gift, you could cut letter shapes from your dough to spell out a special friend's name.

Cheesy niblets

These cheesy niblets are definitely my favourite treat. Sometimes Mum puts a few in my ballet bag for me to eat after lessons and I dance all the way home!

We love cheese!

To make around 30 niblets you will need:

* 100g (3½oz) plain flour
* 75g (2½oz) chilled butter
* 1 egg yolk
* 125g (4oz) Cheddar cheese (grated)

For the topping:

* 1tbsp Parmesan cheese (grated)
* 1 egg
* 1tbsp water

Try to use just your finger tips!

1. Ask an adult to turn the oven on to 200°C (400°F/Gas 6).

2. Sieve the flour into a large mixing bowl. Cut the butter into small chunks and add.

3. With your fingers, rub the butter into the flour until there are no lumps in your mixture.

4. Add the egg yolk
and Cheddar cheese to
the bowl and stir well.

5. Now, using your hands,
gather the mixture together
to form a dough. Your
dough should look like this.

Now turn
the page!

6. Sprinkle a little flour onto a clean worktop and roll out the dough until it is around 5mm thick.

7. Cut out shapes using a biscuit cutter or blunt knife. Place each one carefully on a lightly greased non-stick baking tray.

Triangle shapes look just like little pieces of cheese!

My Dad likes to eat niblets with his tea.

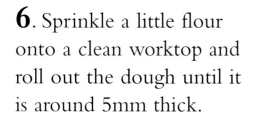

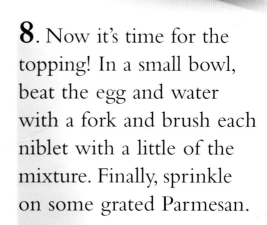

8. Now it's time for the topping! In a small bowl, beat the egg and water with a fork and brush each niblet with a little of the mixture. Finally, sprinkle on some grated Parmesan.

9. Ask an adult to put the niblets in the oven to cook for 15 minutes, or until they are golden.

10. Once the niblets are ready, ask an adult to remove them from the oven and place them on a wire rack to cool.

You can try making little bags from greaseproof paper to put your niblets in!

Mmm – smells good!

13

Sweet creams

Henry has a sweet tooth, so this is his favourite recipe. These vanilla and mint creams are lots of fun to make with friends and are perfect for parties.

I can't wait to make them!

To make around 15 creams you will need:

★ 250g (8oz) icing sugar
★ 1 egg white
★ drop of peppermint essence
★ drop of vanilla essence
★ drop of yellow and drop of green food colouring

1. In a small bowl, beat the egg white with a fork, until it is frothy.

2. Sieve the icing sugar into a medium bowl and add a little of the egg white.

3. With a wooden spoon, stir the mixture well and continue adding the egg white until you have a stiff dough. If the mixture is too runny, add a little more icing sugar.

4. Using your hands, divide the mixture into two and place one half in another bowl. Add the peppermint essence and green food colouring to one bowl, and the vanilla essence and yellow food colouring to the other.

Food colourings are very strong so only add a tiny amount!

5. Knead each mixture with your hands until the flavourings and colours are blended evenly.

6. Sprinkle a little icing sugar onto a clean work surface and roll out your dough. It should be about 3mm thick.

7. Now cut out some pretty shapes using small biscuit cutters.

8. Leave your creams to harden for several hours before eating them – if you can wait that long!

Lovely lemonade

Dancing makes me thirsty!

After practising lots of twirls and pirouettes, a cool glass of lemonade is just perfect. It's fun to drink with a straw and really refreshing when it has been chilled in the fridge.

For 2 litres (3 pints) of lemonade you will need:

★ 6 large unwaxed lemons
★ 150g (5oz) granulated sugar
★ 1.5 litres (2.5 pints) water

1. Wash the lemons in warm water, then remove just the outer part of the skin (zest) from three of them, using a lemon zester or potato peeler.

Try not to remove the white underneath (pith) as this tastes bitter. Put the zest into a large bowl.

2. Next, squeeze all six lemons and add the juice to the zest. Don't worry about the pips! Now add the sugar to the bowl.

3. Ask an adult to boil the water and then pour it into the bowl, stir well with a wooden spoon and cover. Leave overnight in a cool place.

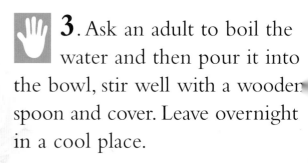

4. The next day, stir the lemonade again and then, using a sieve, strain the liquid into a pretty jug. Leave the jug in the fridge to chill for a few hours.

On sunny days we drink lemonade in the garden!

You can make pink lemonade too! In a bowl, mash some raspberries with a fork and strain the juice into your jug.

Dreamy dips

You'll twirl for these dips!

The best thing about dips is they're so yummy and easy to make after a hard day's dancing. They are great for parties and you and your friends will just love dipping your favourite fruit into these delicious dips!

To make the dips you will need:

★ 150g (5oz) soft cheese
★ 3tbsp Greek yoghurt
★ 3tbsp clear honey
★ 30g (1oz) milk chocolate
★ Selection of fruit for dipping!

1. In a bowl, mix the soft cheese with the Greek yoghurt. Put one half of the mixture into another bowl and add the honey to it.

2. Break the chocolate into pieces and put in a glass bowl. Ask an adult to place the bowl over a pan of simmering water, making sure the bowl doesn't touch the water. When the chocolate has melted, ask an adult to take the bowl off the pan.

3. Ask an adult to help you pour the chocolate into the bowl that contains just the cream cheese and yoghurt, and mix it in well. Take care when you are doing this as the bowl could be quite hot and you may need to wear some oven gloves.

Oooh – berries and dips!

4. Spoon your dips into pretty bowls and serve with a selection of delicious fruit. You could also try dipping other yummy things like biscuits or mini marshmallows!

19

Mini cheese pies

This is my Mum's special pie recipe. Her cheese pies are so delicious, they're famous throughout Chipping Cheddar! When my friends are coming for tea, I help my mum to make them.

I'm a happy baker!

To make about 12 pies you will need:

- ★ 100g (3½oz) ready-made shortcrust pastry
- ★ 1 large egg
- ★ 75g (2½oz) Cheddar cheese
- ★ 30g (1oz) Parmesan cheese
- ★ 5tbsp single cream

1. Ask an adult to turn on the oven to 200°C (400°F/Gas 6).

This part is easy!

2. Roll out your pastry on a floured surface. Now cut out 12 circles with a fluted cutter and fill a bun tin. Put the bun tin in the fridge to chill for about 15 minutes.

3. Collect up the leftover pastry and roll it out again. Using a blunt knife, cut the pastry into thin strips and put them in the fridge to chill.

Make sure the strips are long enough to cover your pies!

4. Using a fork, lightly beat the egg in a medium mixing bowl. Remove about a tablespoon of the beaten egg and put it in a small bowl to use later.

5. Next, grate both kinds of cheese and add to the egg. Stir in the cream and season with a little salt and pepper (optional).

Now turn the page!

6. Take your pastry from the fridge, then use a teaspoon to carefully fill each case with the cheesy mixture.

7. Brush your pastry strips with the beaten egg you set aside before.

8. Lay two strips of pastry across the top of each pie to form a cross.

Have fun making pies!

9. Ask an adult to place the pies in the oven to bake for 15–20 minutes, or until they have set and the pastry is golden.

The cheese pies will be very hot when they have come out of the oven, so leave them to cool for a little while before you try one!

These cheese pies are so scrumptious!

Mrs Mouseling's pies are the best ever!

Strawberry bites

Dancers love special treats!

If you love to nibble berries like me, you'll adore these strawberry bites. They're very dainty and delicate, so they're perfect for special ballerina parties.

To make 20 bites you will need:

★ 2 egg whites
★ 100g (3½oz) caster sugar
★ Pink food colouring (optional)
★ 300ml (½ pint) whipped cream
★ Strawberries to decorate

1. Ask an adult to turn on the oven to 120°C (250°F/Gas ½).

2. Put the egg whites into a large, clean mixing bowl, and whisk them until they are stiff enough to form small peaks. You can use a hand whisk or an electric whisk to do this.

3. Add the sugar to the bowl, one teaspoon at a time, whisking all the time. Soon the mixture will look glossy.

4. You can make pink bites by adding a drop of pink food colouring to the mixture at this stage. Carefully fold it in with a metal spoon so you don't beat the air out of the mixture.

Mum's meringues are lovely and light.

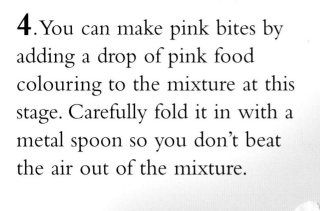

5. Using two teaspoons, place little mounds of mixture onto a baking sheet lined with non-stick parchment paper.

Leave space between each one!

6. Ask an adult to put your bites into the oven to cook for about an hour. When they are done, ask an adult to remove them from the oven and leave them to cool.

7. Place the bites on a plate and top each one with a little whipped cream and a slice of strawberry!

Crispy crunches

Crispy crunches are fun to make and they are my Dad's favourite! When I put on a show at home, crunches make a nice treat for my audience to eat while they watch!

Dad and I love to make crunches!

For around 24 crunches you will need:

★ 100g (3½oz) milk chocolate
★ 30g (1oz) butter
★ 60g (2oz) crisped rice cereal
★ 2tbsp raisins

1. Break the chocolate into pieces and place in a bowl with the butter.

2. Ask an adult to help you rest the bowl on top of a pan of simmering water, making sure the bowl doesn't touch the water. Stir gently until everything has melted.

3. With help from an adult, take the bowl off the pan and stir in the cereal and raisins. Be careful as the bowl will be hot.

I want one!

4. Using a teaspoon, fill tiny paper cases with the mixture and leave them to cool. When they have cooled they are ready to eat!

You can make crispy cranberry crunches too! All you need to do is use good quality white cooking chocolate instead of milk chocolate, and add dried cranberries instead of raisins!

Dainty cakes

These little cakes are light, delicate and so pretty – perfect to share for afternoon tea! They're easy and quick to make, and lots of fun to decorate.

Hooray! My favourite recipe!

For around 12 cakes you will need:

★ 100g (3½oz) self-raising flour
★ 100g (3½oz) caster sugar
★ 100g (3½oz) softened butter
★ 2 eggs
★ 1tsp baking powder
★ 4 drops vanilla essence

Sieving the flour is fun!

1. Ask an adult to turn on the oven to 180°C (350°F/Gas 4). Now put 12 paper cake cases into a bun tin, ready for your mixture.

2. Put all the ingredients into a large mixing bowl. As you add the flour remember to sieve it to remove any lumps.

3. With a wooden spoon, mix everything well. It's quite hard work, so you might need someone to help you stir the mixture until it is light and creamy.

Keep mixing until it's creamy like this.

4. Spoon some of the mixture into each paper case until they are about three-quarters full.

5. Ask an adult to put the cakes into the oven to cook for 15 minutes until they are golden brown and soft and springy!

Now turn the page!

6. When your cakes are ready, ask an adult to take them out of the oven and place them on a cooling rack. Leave them until they are completely cold.

For the icing you will need:

★ 200g (7oz) icing sugar

★ 2tbsp water

★ Food colourings (optional)

7. Now it's time to make the icing! Sieve the icing sugar into a bowl and add the water. Mix together until you have a thick white paste. You can add a little more water if you need to make the icing a bit more runny.

8. If you want to make icing in different colours, spoon small amounts of white icing into little bowls. Now, add a tiny drop of food colouring to each bowl and stir!

Lilac icing is so sweet.

9. Using a different teaspoon for each colour, spread the icing on your cakes.

10. While the icing is still wet, it's time to decorate your cakes. There are lots of pretty things you can use, like sugar strands, little sweets, or ready-made cake decorations you can buy from a shop. When the cakes are ready, they'll look good enough to eat!

Mmm – yummy!

These are perfect for birthday parties!

Acknowledgements

Dorling Kindersley would like to thank the following for their
help in preparing this book:

The children and their parents who attended the photo shoot;
Dave King for his beautiful photographs; Sarah Tildesley for her
invaluable advice and patience during the photo shoot;
Fiona Munro for all her help with the recipes.